Haunted Yorkshire

Introduction

Yorkshire. God's own country. From the beautiful Dales and moors to the breathtaking coastline which has inspired artists and writers throughout the centuries. Not forgetting the weird and wonderful array of fun filled accents (a book could be written on those alone). The county enjoys a rich heritage. Shaped throughout its history by the Celts, Romans and Vikings to name but a few. Housed within the boundaries of this green and pleasant shire is of a portfolio of fascinating historic buildings. Some of which are said to be the location for all kinds of ghoulish hauntings and sinister ghostly sights. Ghosts, poltergeists in fact anything that falls under the umbrella of the *paranormal* can be argued about all day long. In depth debates can rage on and on until the proverbial cows come home (Yorkshire cows of course). Ghosts are they real or not? Was it a gust of wind or an unseen entity that slammed the door? What was that noise, an animal or something else? A weather balloon or a UFO? Regardless of which side of the argument you may fall on one thing is not up for debate and that is the fact that the stories from these haunted Yorkshire buildings have stood the test of time. From chilling Roman armies to spooky dead monks, gruesome murdered maids and chilling crying babies, these ghostly Yorkshire landmarks are not for the faint-hearted. Are you brave enough to read about them and maybe even pay them a visit?

The following locations are by no means the *only* buildings which have paranormal mysteries attached to them. Yorkshire is full of buildings each with their own grizzly tales to tell. A book containing each and everyone of them would be quite a volume! The following places are however a collection of sites that are both spooky and intriguing. I have visited most of them personally and aim to grace the others with my presence as soon as possible!

Contents

Chapter 1- York

Chapter 2- Abbey's & Churches

Chapter 3- Halls and Manors

Chapter 4- Hotels

Chapter 5- Theatres

Chapter 6- Pubs

Chapter 7- Castles

Chapter 1

York

This ancient walled city sits beside the River Ouse and dates as far back as 71AD. Naturally over the years it has seen its fair share of blood shed, murder, and tragedy. So much has occurred here, that really York demands a book of its own let alone a single chapter but we are going to look at some of the cities greatest haunted locations.

The Treasurer's House at York Minster is now a National Trust museum. The Grade-I listed building was originally built on the site of a Roman road. Up until 1547, the 'Treasurer's House' was the home for the Treasurer's of York Minster, an incredibly important job, essentially looking after the finances of the Churches in the area. They also entertained the important guests of the church and the nearby towns, so a sumptuous dwelling was deemed appropriate. After the reformation of the English church, the job of Treasurer no longer existed, so the house was given to the archbishops of the community, and then subsequently into private ownership. It played host to the families of the upper classes and then finally, in 1893, then it came into the hands of Frank Green, who restored the now tired looking house.

Green used the house as a display for his collection of antiques and other valuables, and turned each room into a host for his collections of different eras, and different periods in history.

In 1930 Green handed the Treasurer's House and its contents to the National Trust. Skip forward 23 years to 1953. A young 18-year-old plumbing apprentice named Harry Martindale, was fixing a pipe in the cellar when he heard a musical sound. Thinking nothing of it he continued on with his work. The sound continued and it grew closer and closer. Eventually Harry looked down and saw nine or ten pairs of Roman soldiers marching with trumpets past the bottom of his ladder. If seeing this wasn't odd enough the peculiarity of the situation was boosted even more by the soldiers appearing to be walking on their knees. The Romans legs disappeared into the floor of the cellar. However, as the soldiers marched into an excavated trench further in the cellar, their full legs came into view. The soldiers were, in fact, walking at the level of the original old Roman Road!

Soon the Romans passed through the opposite wall from where they appeared. But Harry could hear more sounds. A horse came into view next, and sitting atop it was another soldier, in full military uniform, but this time holding a round shield on his left arm. The horse made its way across the room and also disappeared into the opposite wall.

More soldiers on foot followed, walking in pairs. By this time Harry was absolutely terrified and understandably was unable to count exactly how many there were, but has been quoted as stating he saw at least twenty. Mr Martindale also stated that the soldiers were talking to each other in whispers, and their faces seemed to be sad or tired. The uniforms, from what he could tell, seemed to be covered in mud. All were armed either with spears or swords. They all looked as solid as any other person. Naturally Harry ran from the cellar the second the last soldier disappeared.

Interestingly an elderly gentleman who was in charge of the house took one look at Harry and said 'You have seen the soldiers, haven't you?' Also the caretaker of the property had seen the soldiers the previous year, but had not told anyone for fear of ridicule. Harry left the house and did not return for at least 25 years. Four years later another person, a new caretaker of the house, witnessed the soldiers in exactly the same manner as Harry had – all walking in pairs except for one astride his horse. That was the last time the soldiers were seen.

Two points of interest should be noted here. The first is that Harry Martindale was accused of lying about the incident due to the description he gave regarding the colours of the soldiers' uniforms and also the style of their weapons. However, in the 1990's and into the 2000's, archaeological digs of old Roman forts along Hadrian's Wall (at one time the most heavily fortified borders in the Roman Empire) uncovered many remnants of the Romans who were once stationed there. Amongst them, parts of uniforms belonging to Roman auxiliary soldiers, that exactly matched the descriptions given by Harry Martindale, nearly half a century earlier, right down to the colour of the leathers and the size and shape of the shields.

A second note is that Harry said he had never seen a ghost before that day in the cellar and that he has never seen one since. To me these words from Martindale add a real ring of truth to the incident. If you fancy a trip to the Treasurer's House it can be found at the below address.

Treasurer's House, Minster Yard, York, North Yorkshire, YO1 7JL.

York Minster is arguably York's most famous building, it is a breathtaking sight to behold and the current building is believed to date all the way back to 627. There have been churches and forts on this site throughout the centuries. Constantine was declared Emperor from the Roman settlement here in 306. The ruins of which can still be seen in the basement of the Minster and are certainly worth a visit! With such a long history behind the building it is not surprising that York Minster is considered to be one of the most haunted places in York.

The spirit of one of the architects of the Minster has been reported on a number of occasions. He is said to appear looking up at the stone work inside the building wearing a white hat.

Another spirit said to haunt York Minster is a young man believed to be Dean Gale who died in 1702 aged 26. His ghostly apparition has been reported sitting in the pews and listening to the sermons. There are also reports of a ghostly choir boy who joins in for a sing song! There have also been sightings of monks and an arsonist who had set fire to the Minster back in the 19th Century.

A lovely story that is often shared about the Minster dates back to the 1820s when two members of a tour group were separated from the crowd and found themselves wandering alone through the building. On their wanderings they encountered a man in a naval uniform. The man approached the ladies and whispered in one of their ears before walking off. The story goes that he was actually the woman's brother and they had made a pact that whoever died first had to come and tell the other if there really was an afterlife. After dying at sea the brother came back to keep his promise to his sister!

35 Stonegate.

Over the years, 35 Stonegate has become known as York's most haunted building. It is a building that is soaked in history and it is certainly very atmospheric. It is quite a magnificent medieval building with a variety of rooms of different sizes. The current house was built in 1482 although records show that some form of structure or house has occupied that site for at least 1000 years. For over 200 years, the building was the home to the publishing house "The Sign of the Bible". This house is said to have at least 14 different ghosts, but many believe that there are actually many more! A couple are said to be in one of the back rooms and a distraught lady who hangs around in the kitchen. Many of them became active in the late nineties when the property was heavily renovated suggesting that the work stirred them a pattern we will see often throughout this book. Prompting the owner at the time to state..."Suddenly we couldn't move for spectral figures...It was like Piccadilly Circus." As work digging in the foundations got underway.

One of the most documented spirits of 35 Stonegate is known simply as Tom and he seems to occupy the Seance Room second floor. Other paranormal activity includes the figure of a balding monk seen in the Lantern Room, and an apparition of an elegant Georgian Lady seen in the Dining Room. Doors opening and shutting with accompanying bangs and creaks are heard by visitors when alone in the house. Visitors have also felt the icy touch of invisible fingers and heard eerie screeching from the attic.

Marmaduke Buckle House.

One of York's saddest ghost stories must be the one of Marmaduke Buckle. He was physically handicapped and in the 17th Century that condition led to him being accused of witchcraft. He spent most of his life in the house on Goodramgate which is now the La Piazza restaurant, until one day he could take the wrath of the people of York no more.

Marmaduke carved his initials, birth date (1697) and that day's date (1715) on a beam, and ended his short tragic life by hanging himself from the beam. The carvings are still present today. His ghost is alleged to still roam round both buildings, and his presence has even been accused of trying to push somebody down the stairs in the pub next door, although more usually he is said to close doors and turn lights on and off.

Chapter 2

Abbey's & Churches

Bolton Abbey is one of the only surviving examples of an Augustinian monastery in the UK. It was ruined after the Dissolution of the Monasteries but the destruction hasn't stopped it from being one of the most haunted buildings in Yorkshire. It's said that the existing structures are haunted by the ghost of a monk who died just before the Dissolution and his soul has never been able to rest. He's been named the Black Canon thanks to his dark cassock, cloak and hat – you can even hear his footsteps wandering around the rectory. It was apparently first witnessed by the Marquis of Hartington in 1912, who provided a very good description of the apparition. Also the smell of incense burning is often reported by visitors to the site.

Bolton Abbey, Skipton, North Yorkshire, BD23 6AL.

Fountains Abbey & Hall Ripon

Fountains Abbey is one of the most popular attractions in Yorkshire, a ruined Cistercian monastery full of beautiful relics of a bygone era, but it's also one of the most haunted. There have been reports of a ghostly choir chanting in the Chapel of Nine Altars and an Elizabethan man emerging from the panelling in the Fountains Hall. The spirit of the daughter of Sir Stephen Proctor, who built Fountains Hall in the 16th century, is believed to roam the halls too.

Fountains Abbey & Hall, Ripon, North Yorkshire, HG4 3DY.

Whitby Abbey

The coastal town of Whitby boasts a rich history. Nautical titans such as Captain Cook are connected with the town as are smugglers and pirates. Whitby also famously inspired Bram Stoker's Gothic novel *Dracula.* One of the harbour towns more dramatic features is the ruined Abbey that sits high above Whitby seemingly dominating the town.

Once-great a Benedictine monastery, founded in the 11th century. The medieval abbey stands on the site of a much earlier monastery, founded in 657 by an Anglian princess, Hild, who became its first abbess.

Many sightings of a ghostly nun have been documented over the years. It is said that she was bricked up in the dungeons. Also the ghost of the abbey's founder, St. Hild, has been reported gazing out from the windows.

Other Whitby hauntings include a ghostly coach that plunges over the cliff edge on its way to church, an entity that stalks the roads damaging cars and road signs. The apparitions of a pirate, children playing and phantoms of men and women are said to stalk various parts of the old seafaring town. Appearing briefly to unsuspecting visitors in the Whitby's narrow lanes.

Monk Bretton Priory & The Mill of The Black Monk

Founded in 1154 as the Priory of St. Mary Magdelene of Lund by Adam Fitswane, sited on the Lund, prompting a nearby village to be named Lundwood. In the course of time the priory took the name of the nearby village of Bretton to be commonly known as Monk Bretton Priory.

The monastery fell victim to Henry VIII dissolution, surrendering to Thomas Cromwell on 30 November 1538 and the site passed into the ownership of the Blithman family. In 1580 the land was again sold to George Talbot, 6th Earl of Shrewsbury who gave the estate to his fourth son Henry on his marriage to Elizabeth Rayner. The site is a Scheduled Ancient Monument and now in the care of English Heritage. The site still has the remains of monks buried there.

The vague shapes of men in long gowns have been seen running around this area. Especially by residents living close to the ruins of the Priory. I have a personal story to share regarding this site. I visited the Priory on the 30th of November 2018 the 480th anniversary of the Priory closing. I was taking some pictures when I felt the hood of my large brown jumper being pulled not tugged gently PULLED! I am also what some people call follically challenged leaving me bald on the top of my head with bits around the sides. Had my robe like hoodie and my haircut given a spirit the impression I was a monk? Maybe it was a Monk attempting to pull me to safety from the King's men who had come to close the Priory. Possibly it could have been that of a guard mistaking me for a Monk and pulling me away from the Priory.

Near the priory is the Mill of the Black Monks, which claims to be the oldest inn in England, which some people say is also haunted.

This ancient building in Cundy Cross, just outside Barnsley, was originally a watermill. Built in 1150 by the Cluniac Monks from nearby Monk Bretton Priory, it passed into the hands of the Benedictines, and in the 17th century the mill was taken over by the Quakers.

The building lay in ruins for many years before extensive renovations returned its former glory, and today it is a beautiful roadside tavern. It still houses an original wooden door. Rather than its haunted history putting off the drinkers, psychic experts who have claimed to be in contact with the Mill's several ghosts have encouraged the curious to visit. Conversion work, which began in 1991, saw a number of disturbances - a common factor in hauntings. Barmaids have described how unseen hands have touched them, and white shapes have floated through the walls. Customers have seen small objects such as ashtrays and glasses move of their own free will and even fly across the room. The figure of a 'solid-looking' ghostly monk standing in the shadows has manifested itself on several occasions.

Monk Bretton Priory, Abbey Lane, Barnsley, S715QD

Nostell Priory, Wakefield, West Yorkshire

Located just a stone's throw from Monk Bretton Priory close to Wakefield in West Yorkshire, is this 18th century palladian house and of course it has it's very own ghost, known as Nancy. Nancy was a maid who worked at the house, who died in the 1920s by decapitation after putting her head into a lift shaft to see where the next car was.

Nostell Priory workers know Nancy well and even class her as part of the team. Visitors also claim to see her from time to time on their tours.

It appears Nancy is a rather friendly ghost with a kindly nature so even the most timid paranormal fan will be safe here!

Chapter 3

Halls and Manors

Now split into three living spaces, the Grade-II listed Hodroyd Hall on the outskirts of Barnsley. It has existed in some form since the 12th century and many spirits are believed to reside within it. Over the years, there have been sightings of a nun, a monk, shadows that appear in empty corridors and a faceless man known as Dr Bell on the main staircase, but the most gruesome of all is that of the apparition of a murdered kitchen maid who was killed and burnt in one of old fireplaces at Hodroyd Hall. She is said to want to make her presence known to visitors.

Hodroyd Hall, Kirkgate Lane, South Hiendley, Barnsley, South Yorkshire, S72 9DR.

Bolling Hall

Built on a commanding hillside in the 14th century, Bolling Hall is one of the oldest buildings in Bradford. It sits roughly a mile from the city center and it even has a mention in the Domesday Book, under the ownership of a man named Sindi. It's now a museum and education centre, but it was used as a home for over 500 years and the hall is reputed to have at least 20 ghosts in that time, the earliest dating back to the 1600s. This early haunting was reported by the Earl of Newcastle, who was stationed at the hall after his troops took over the Town of Bradford. He reported that his bed cover had been tugged waking to see a woman wringing her hands, telling him to "pity poor Bradford". It was the Earls original intention to devastate the town, but after this spooky experience he changed his mind, and instead ordered his troops to only kill those who offered resistance resulting in just a handful of deaths rather than a mass slaughter.

Footsteps being heard frequently and shadows swiftly darting past you it is difficult not to feel terrified here. Both of these happened to me during a night in the Hall!

A Child's crib has been witnessed on many occasions to rock back and forth as people enter the room. Also a lady dressed in white has been seen, appearing to float in mid air across the room and disappearing into the fireplace in what is called the Blue Room.

Bolling Hall often hosts Paranormal Investigation nights and I'd recommend going along to one.

Bolling Hall, Bolling Hall Road, Bradford, West Yorkshire, BD4 7LP.

Burton Agnes Hall

A stunning Elizabethan manor house near Driffield East Yorkshire. Burton Agnes Hall has more to it than beautiful rooms and landscaped gardens. Built between 1598 and 1610 by Sir Henry Griffith.

A touching yet tragic tale is related to this haunted building. The ghost of Katherine (Anne) Griffith, who died at Burton Agnes Hall in 1620, is reputed to haunt the Queen's State Bedroom. Anne Griffith was the youngest of the three sisters whose portrait hangs in the Inner Hall, daughters of Sir Henry Griffith who built the Hall. The story is that Anne had watched the building of the new house and could talk and think of nothing else; so amazed was she by its splendor. When it was almost finished Anne went one afternoon to visit the St. Quintins at Harpham about a mile away, but near St. John's Well she was attacked and robbed by ruffians. She was brought home to Burton Agnes but was so badly hurt that she died a few days afterwards.

She told her sisters that she would never rest unless part of her could remain in 'our beautiful home as long as it shall last'. She made them promise that when she was dead her head should be severed and preserved in the Hall forever, and to pacify her, the sisters agreed. However when Anne died, her body was buried in the churchyard.

Her spirit was said to have begun to roam the house shortly after, naturally terrifying everyone! Remembering Anne's dying words, the sisters took counsel with the vicar and eventually it was agreed that the grave should be opened. The skull was brought into the house and so long as it was undisturbed, the Hall was at peace and untroubled. However many attempts have been made to get rid of it over the years. Once it was thrown away, another time it was buried in the garden, but after every attempt there always followed the ghost walking the house, causing tremendous noise and upheaval. Today the skull is still believed to be in the house, built into one of the old walls, probably in the Great Hall. Nobody knows for sure just where it is but now she can watch over 'her beautiful home'.

Burton Agnes Hall, Rudston Road, Burton Agnes, Driffield, East Yorkshire, YO25 4NB.

East Riddlesden Hall

Built all the way back in the 1630s, the 17th Century East Riddlesden Hall has a long history full of comings, goings, births, and deaths. It is said that the building has been the site of paranormal activity for several hundred years, and even today the National Trust still receives fresh reports of spooky goings-on.

Most workers of East Riddlesden Hall have at some point experienced an unexplainable event or ghostly encounter. In fact, they occur so much it has been said that a month does not go by without some significant paranormal activity occurring. A ghost hunter's dream come true!

A regular spirit at the hall is The Grey Lady, who is often encountered by children rather than adults. Her presence reputedly stems from the civil war, when the man of the house returned from battle to discover his wife had been having an affair – so he killed the lover and bricked-up his wife behind a wall to slowly die.

Many of these children don't realise the building has a reputation for being haunted, they often ask the tour guides about "the lady in the corner", only for the guide to turn and find nobody there.

Along with the school children who visit Riddlesden Hall there are said to be a number of ghostly juveniles residing in the building. One of the most infamous stories of East Riddlesden Hall concerns a member of staff who noticed a small boy wandering around the building in period clothing. School groups often visit the Hall in costume. Believing the boy to be a member of such a school group, she approached the child and asked him if he had become separated from his class. After receiving no answer from the boy, the woman went to the office to report the incident, at which point she was informed that no school groups were visiting that day.

There are also reports of a cradle rocking on it's own and the figure of a Catholic priest.

East Riddlesden Hall, Bradford Rd, Riddlesden, Keighley BD20 5EL

Chapter 4

Hotels

Built in 1890, The Midland Hotel is a classic example of a Victorian railway hotel, but not all the guests will get a good night's sleep here. Dracula author Bram Stoker visited Bradford to see his friend Sir Henry Irving perform at the Theatre Royal, only for Irving to collapse during the show. He was rushed to the lobby of the hotel where he died and it's his apparition that has been spotted in a smoky haze in the room he slept in the night before his final performance. Also a night porter has reportedly been seen going about his business.

The Midland Hotel, Forster Square, Bradford, West Yorkshire, BD1 4HU.

Dean Court

Back we go to York to the Dean Court Hotel. It has been the scene of some strange goings-on in the past, including the apparition of a Roman Soldier. Sat in the shadow of York Minster and now a Best Western property, it was built in 1855 across three buildings, and housed the Clergy of the Minster. A frequent saying is heard about this hotel...If you do book a room, try to avoid room 36! That's where most of the paranormal activity has occurred. Reports of slamming doors, guests feeling pressure on their chests as they lay in bed sleeping, objects moving around and unusual cold spots even in summer. There's also the ghost known as the Mad Maid — who has reportedly told mediums she used to clean the guest house next door, which is now part of Dean Court Hotel.

Bagdale Hall. Whitby.

Dating from back to around 1516, this old building is reputedly the eternal home of Browne Bushell, a former navy officer who was executed for treason in 1651. This Tudor manor house is thought to be the oldest building still standing in Whitby and former owner Browne Bushell is said to still roam its corridors. He's been spied walking up and down staircases, while poltergeist activity and the sounds of whispering voices and a crying child have also been heard. Sleep tight!

Crown Hotel.

Situated to the south of Doncaster in Bawtry. The Crown Hotel was built for the heavy coaching traffic and as a posting house. It is supposedly haunted by a variety of apparitions. Witnesses have reported seeing an aged monk in a belted habit, who haunts the stables. It was there that he died many years ago. Wandering the dining rooms is the ghost of a young waitress. Her lover took life in a fit of temper and rage. Dick Turpin who certainly gets about in spirit form has been reported to have been seen in the bar. A young child has been witnessed by a psychic, sitting in the corner of the restaurant. Finally, there is the Crinoline Lady who died in a fire many years ago in the old wing.

Mosborough Hall Hotel.

This hotel, (now run by Best Western), sits just 15 minutes from Chesterfield, Sheffield and the Peak District. It is steeped in history. Originally a 12th century manor house. Resident ghosts include the White Lady, a governess at the hall who found herself pregnant with the squire's baby. He had promised to care for her and provide her with a small cottage to live in. He reneged on his promise and it is said you sometimes hear their final argument. The governess threatened to tell the squire's wife, and he slit her throat. There's also the story of Dr Pilcher, a doctor who treated the army detachment who stayed at the hall at the turn of the 20th century. Dismissing the story of the White Lady, he braved a night in the room where she died. The next morning an attendant came in with a cup of tea, both he and Doctor were horrified to turn and see the sheets and pillowcase dripping with blood. He resigned from his role and never set foot in Mosborough Hall again! The Hotel actually offers a Haunted Ghost Package night in the Lord John Darcy Suite the scene of these grim tales.

Chapter 5

Theatres

Old Georgain Theatre.

Richmond, a historic market town close to Catterick in North Yorkshire is home to one of the oldest theatres in the land, The Georgian Theatre Royal. The Georgian playhouse was built in 1788 by the actor-manager Samuel Butler and his first wife Tryphosa Butler. In it's time the place has been used not only as a theatre but as an auction house and storage facility too. It is unclear when the hauntings first began but during heavy renovation work in 2002 right up until the present day the spirit of a man has been seen to cross the stage many believing it to be Samuel Butler still treading the boards in his beloved theatre.

Theatre Royal, Bradford.

So not only do we have reports of Sir Henry Irving haunting the hotel where he died. There are also reports of his manifestation appearing at the Theatre Royal in Bradford where he performed the night he died.

Hull New Theatre

Hull New Theatre opened on Saturday, October 16, 1939 with Noel Gay's 'Me And My Girl'. The car park behind the theatre was once home to Christchurch, where both Lewis Carroll's mother's parents were married and "Jack the Ripper" suspect Dr. Frederick Richard Chapman also got married there.

The theatre has played host to a wide range of celebrities over its history including Laurel and Hardy in July 1947. Charles Dickens also made appearances, reading his books to a captive audience.

The theatre is not shy about the resident ghosts. One of the most well known of the spirits said to reside in the building is that of "Charlie," a mischievous spirit said to knock on doors, open and close doors and cause chaos down in the dressing rooms. In the 80's the musical comedy version of A Christmas Carol was interrupted by a fire alarm which was attributed to "Charlie".

A lady has been seen in the dress circle, and a general feeling of unease has been reported. People have also reported being scratched whilst in Royal Box B.

Leeds City Varieties.

This Grade II listed music hall was built in 1865 as an adjunct to the White Swan Inn (dating from 1748) in Swan Street and it's original interior is largely unaltered. It is one of the few remaining examples of the Victorian era music halls of the 1850s/1860s. The theatre was founded by local pub landlord and benefactor Charles Thornton and was originally called 'Thornton's New Music Hall and Fashionable Lounge'. Again we see activity beginning to occur when refurbishments on the building were taking place (in this case they began 2011).

There are a number of strange tales, from the sound of a piano playing music well into the night. Also reports of knocking and banging in the main bar have been witnessed. A red-haired woman is said to patrol the theatre when performances are on – it's said that when she's seen, it can indicate if a show will be successful. However who this woman could be nobody knows.

The oddest rumour, however, is that paranormal activity is believed to affect the paintings adorning the walls, becoming warped.

30 East Drive, Pontefract.

Ok this next location isn't a theatre but I couldn't miss it out. 30 East Drive in Pontefract. From the outside it looks to be a normal semi-detached house but on the inside it has seen a lot of paranormal activity. The events of the house inspired the film, *When The Lights Go Out.* Said to be haunted by a young girl and a demonic Cluniac monk who was hung for rape during the time of Henry VIII. Poltergeist phenomena are frequent in this house with furniture being moved, plates being thrown and people being pushed down the stairs. The pushing of people down the stairs became such a problem that the people who ran Paranormal Investigations there demanded that everyone hold on to the stair rail when moving up and down the stairs. Other inexplicable events include; green foam appearing from taps and toilet even after the water was turned off, the tea dispenser being activated resulting in all the dried tea cascading onto the work surface, lights being turned off and on. It truly is a very haunted location!

Chapter 6

Pubs

The Fleece Inn.

The television programme, Most Haunted, named The Fleece Inn in Elland the most haunted pub in Britain and there are many incredibly chilling tales from this 400-year old ale house. There have been reports of murders, secret tunnels and headless horsemen at the pub, its current landlords have their own tales of a poltergeist. From glasses falling off shelves to shadowy figures moving between rooms, an evening here may require a stiff drink!

The Fleece Inn, Westgate, Elland, West Yorkshire, HX5 0BB.

Carbrook Hall.

Carbrook Hall has been known for many years as one of the most haunted pubs in Yorkshire. Located in the Attercliffe district of Sheffield. The original building was owned by the Blunt family from 1176. Rebuilt in 1462, and was bought by Thomas Bright (Lord of the manor of Ecclesall) in the late 16th century. His descendant, John Bright, was an active Parliamentarian during the English Civil War, and the building was used as a Roundhead meeting place during the siege of Sheffield Castle. Most of the building was demolished in the 19th century, what survives is a Grade II listed stone wing that was added circa 1620. In 2019 Starbucks opened a Drive Through Coffee House on the site which maintains all the original features including the plaster mouldings and wood panelling. It is reputed to be haunted with the sounds of children and babies crying and a number of doors opening on their own. The spirit of John Blunt, who owned the pub when Oliver Cromwell used it for meetings in the 1640s, roams the halls as does one of an elderly woman wearing 1920s clothes. Be wary of the ladies' loos, there's a mischievous ghost who makes leaving the cubicles impossible.

Carbrook Hall, 537 Attercliffe Common, Sheffield, South Yorkshire, S9 2FJ.

The Ye Olde Starre Inne. This old coaching inn dates back to around 1644, although its cellars are thought to date back much further. The cellars are actually the focal point for the hauntings here as many people have reported hearing the screams emanating from there. Historical records show that the cellars were used as makeshift hospitals for the soldiers during the English Civil War. So perhaps it could be the sound of wounded Royalist soldiers crying out for help not realising they are dead. I was interviewing a barmaid here before writing this book and she told me (whilst pulling me a pint, would have been rude not to have one) that she had heard a whisper in the Cellar although she couldn't make out what the whisper said. She had also heard doors rattling on calm nights.

Some of the other paranormal activity linked to Ye Olde Starre Inne includes the old lady dressed in black who is often seen descending the staircase from the upper floors and the two ghostly black cats who are seen in the corner of patrons eyes around the bar. Local legend states that the cats were bricked up inside a pillar that stands between the door and the bar. Adding weight to this tale is the many reports of visitors bringing their dogs into the bar only for them to growl and snarl at the pillar. One dog even managed to knock himself out rushing at the pillar! The practice of bricking up cats in a building is a superstitious one found all across Yorkshire which is said to protect a building against both fire and ill luck.

The Cardigan Arms-Leeds

This Victorian pub is reportedly home to the ghost of an elderly woman, with greyish white hair, who haunts the female toilets, with numerous visitors claiming she has appeared in the reflection of the bathroom mirror.

364 Kirkstall Rd, Burley, Leeds LS4 2HQ

Hales Bar-Harrogate

Hales Bar on Crescent Road was built in the 17th century and is the oldest licensed building in Harrogate. William Hales, purchased the old public house in 1882 and named it after himself. Since reopening as Hales Bar in the 19th century, several instances of paranormal activity have been reported. And the activity persists to this day. The unnerving sound of cackling, maniacal laughter had been reported echoing throughout the bar even when it is empty. Glasses and bottles have been witnessed spinning around on shelves only to fall to the floor, but very strangely they never shatter when they hit the floor.

Customers, and staff, have reported glimpsing strange black shadows walking about the bar at all hours of the day. The bar regulars call the ghost 'Mary' and believe she causes much of the activity in the bar.

Our last stop takes us to The Black Swan on the very fringes of York. A renowned pub, hotel and restaurant that dates back over 500 years in Helmsley. It actually consists of 3 different buildings: a black and white timber framed house, a Georgian house and Elizabethan house. The Elizabethan part is believed to occupy the site where the original historic inn stood for many centuries. Notable guests that are alleged to have stayed at the inn was William Wordsworth. Over that time, it's earned a reputation as one of the most haunted places in Yorkshire thanks to a few resident ghosts which have been reported by both staff and guests.

Both have reported seeing a well dressed, older man around the hotel and also the spirit of a young blonde woman as well! There is also a pair of legs with no body attached seen in the private quarter on occasion. I don't know about you but I'd love to see that! The Black Swan can be found at…

The Black Swan, Market Place, Helmsley, York, North Yorkshire, YO62 5BJ.

Chapter 7

Castles

Hazlewood Castle

Hazlewood Castle in Tadcaster is located very close to where the most bloody battle in English history took place - an estimated 30,000 souls perished on March the 29th, 1461 during the notorious Battle of Towton Moor.

Coming from the exit from St Margaret's courtyard, a black dressed figure is reportedly seen walking and disappearing into a yew tree. The same figure has been seen to cross the courtyard from St Margaret's and into the laundry store area.

A priest is believed to have walked from the direction of the Great Hall into the Library before disappearing (they used to walk from the Great Hall to the tower to go down into the cloisters i.e. where the fireplace is now positioned in the Library).

In another part of the Castle in the Lavender bedroom - one of the housekeepers was kneeling down facing the mirror in the bedroom, which faces the bathroom, she became aware of someone in the bathroom and began a conversation believing another housekeeper was there, with no reply. She looked only to find there was no-one there! Also in the Rose bedroom a shadow movement on the wall of a lady looking up the corridor to Jasmine bedroom has been witnessed.

One Christmas a guest complained repeatedly overnight of a baby crying which kept her awake. No babies were in the adjoining rooms

Richmond Castle

Richmond Castle

Rising above the River Swale, Richmond Castle was built by Alan the Red between 1070 and 1086. Although the castle did not serve a significant role in English history, it holds a few secrets …

Legends suggest secret underground passages exist between the castle and Easby Abbey, located a few miles down river. Stories of a ghostly drummer boy still playing his drums surfaced after he disappeared in the hidden tunnels long ago never to be seen again.

Richmond Castle is said to serve as the resting place of King Arthur and his Knights of the Round Table. Presumably, they lie sleeping below the castle walls in a cavern awaiting the day when they will come back to defend the realm in England's greatest time of need.

An additional legend relates to King Arthur and The Knights of the Round Table.

There once lived a man named Potter Thompson whose wife was somewhat of a harridan. To escape her carping one day, Potter went for a long walk where he eventually found himself along the River

Swale, just below Richmond Castle. As he stopped for a rest, Potter noticed an opening in the rocks below the castle. Upon investigating and peering inside, he noticed a long passageway with a faint light in the distance. Potter entered and proceeded towards the light, where he found himself in a cavern surrounded by a sleeping king and his knights who were dressed in full armor. Potter instantly recognized the royal figure as King Arthur due to the horn and legendary sword Excalibur, which were both resting on a nearby table.

Excited by his find, Potter decided to take Excalibur so he could prove to everyone that his story was true. However, as he started to remove the sword from its scabbard, the sleeping knights began to stir. Consequently, Potter became scared and quickly decided to leave the cave. Upon his departure, he heard a sorrowful voice say:

"Potter Thompson, Potter Thompson

If Thou hadst either drawn

The sword, or blown the horn,

Thou wouldst have been the luckiest man

That ever yet was born"

Once outside and able to regain his composure, Potter turned back towards the entrance for another attempt, only to discover the entrance disappeared. He frantically searched the rocky banks of the castle but never again located the secret entrance once revealed to him.

Pontefract Castle

The ruins of Pontefract Castle can be found in the town of Pontefract, in West Yorkshire, England. King Richard II is reported to have died here and it was the site of a series of famous sieges during the 17th-century English Civil War. Tourists visiting the castle from all parts of the world have reported the same sighting, that of a black monk walking from the remains of the kitchen towards the steps of the Queen's Tower. Strangely the monk is always seen walking from west to east, never in the opposite direction. Another unusual thing is the timings of these sightings. The sightings usually take place around 5pm (locking-up time in winter). The Castle's also has an underground magazine, built originally as the cellar for the Great Hall and later used to hold prisoners during the English Civil War. Knocking has been heard coming from this area.

Staff at Pontefract Castle also claim to have witnessed a shadow going down the stairs toward the magazine. Another ghostly inhabitant of the castle is said to be a girl, probably between 9 and 13-years-old, with long brown hair and ragged clothes. She has been spotted in the reflections of the mirror at the visitor's centre on more than one occasion but when the spectator looks round there isn't anybody there…

Sandal castle

Sandal Castle was key in the Battle of wakefield on 30th December 1460. Soldiers killed at the battle are said to be seen wandering the ruins of the castle and the surrounding fields at sunset.

Also there is believed to be at this site a spooky hound called 'cryptid' - a creature whose existence is unverified. Famous cryptids in folklore include yetis and the Loch Ness monster. Many locals have reported seeing this and one woman claims to have photographed it.

Conisbrough Castle

Conisbrough Castle is located close to Doncaster in Conisbrough, South Yorkshire. The stone keep was built approximately 1180 by Hamelin Plantagenet on the site of an earlier wooden structure. Curtain walls were built around the keep in the early 1200s. The keep, which is one of the finest in surviving ones in England, avoided destruction during the English Civil War.

Conisbrough Castle did not play a significant role in history other than an occasional siege through the years. Nonetheless, the castle currently serves as home to a few ghostly residents ...

The ghost of a gray monk has been seen wandering among the ruin curtain walls. There is also the ghost of the "White Lady" who has been seen at the top of the keep, where she was allegedly pushed over the edge to her death.

Unknown footsteps have been heard in the keep. In addition, strange moving lights have been reported from the chapel area of the castle.

Ripley Castle

Ripley Castle is a Grade I listed 14th-century country house and has been the seat of the Ingleby baronets for centuries. The castle is reputedly haunted by the apparition of a rather polite nun who knocks on bedroom doors. However, she will only enter if the room's occupant says, "Come in".

There is also very chilling evidence of the Castle's more bloody history on its walls. Cromwell had opposition soldiers shot against a wall after the Battle of Marston Moor during the civil war the holes in the stone of the building can still be seen to this day. Recently the Castle had a mystery poltergeist hiding candle sticks and then returning them!

That was a short look at some of Yorkshire's most haunted buildings. I certainly hope you enjoyed this book and I really do encourage you to visit these sites. This book has merely scratched the surface of Haunted Yorkshire. The information of the sites was up to date at the time of writing and hopefully nothing has changed too drastically since! Yorkshire is such a wonderful and magical place full of ghosts, myths and legends so look out for other books about the haunted tales of Yorkshire.

Coming soon from this author....

Haunted York- A full book exploring in depth the haunted locations of the ancient city of York.

Yorkshire Myths and Folk Tales- Exploring Yorkshires ancient myths and legends.

Beira- The author's first novel is expected May 2020. Scott is forced to leave his home in Manchester and hide away in the Highlands of Scotland. He is saved by Clara after falling from a mountain side in a snowstorm but his saviour soon becomes his Jailer.

Out Now from this author:

How To Win A White Collar Boxing Match- A guide book for anyone contemplating taking part in a charity boxing match.

The Driving In Cars Monologues- A collection of audition monologues that can be performed from a seat.

Printed in Great Britain
by Amazon